YOUNG GENIUS

BONES

For Ace Rockman — K. L.
To Mum and Dad — E. G.

First edition for the United States, its dependencies,
the Philippines, and Canada published in
2007 by Barron's Educational Series, Inc.

First published in 2006 in Great Britain by Hutchinson,
an imprint of Random House Children's Books

All inquiries should be addressed to:
Barron's Educational Series, Inc.
250 Wireless Boulevard
Hauppauge, New York 11788
www.barronseduc.com

Library of Congress Control Number: 2006932167

ISBN-13: 978-0-7641-3669-6
ISBN-10: 0-7641-3669-0

Printed in China
9 8 7 6 5 4 3 2 1

Hello!
I'm **Young Genius**.

I've been looking into the human body, and all the interesting parts that make it work.

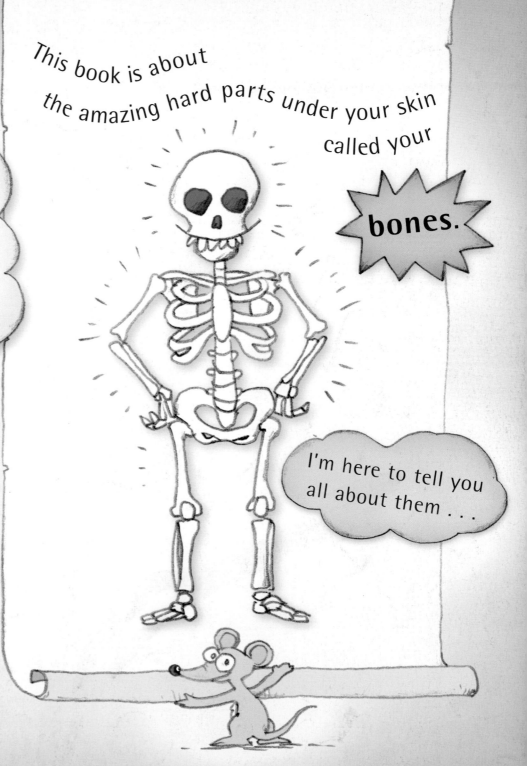

This book is about the amazing hard parts under your skin called your

bones.

I'm here to tell you all about them . . .

Inside your body,
under your skin,
is an amazing machine
called your
skeleton.

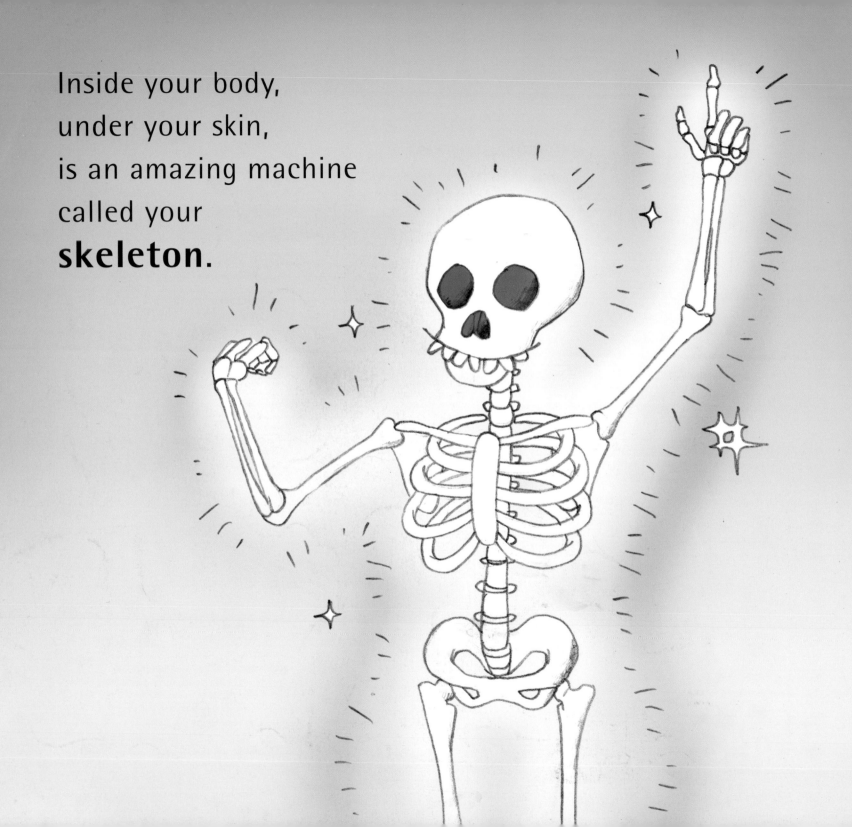

Your skeleton is made up of knobbly white sticks called **bones.**

And they fit together to make a frame that your insides can stick to.

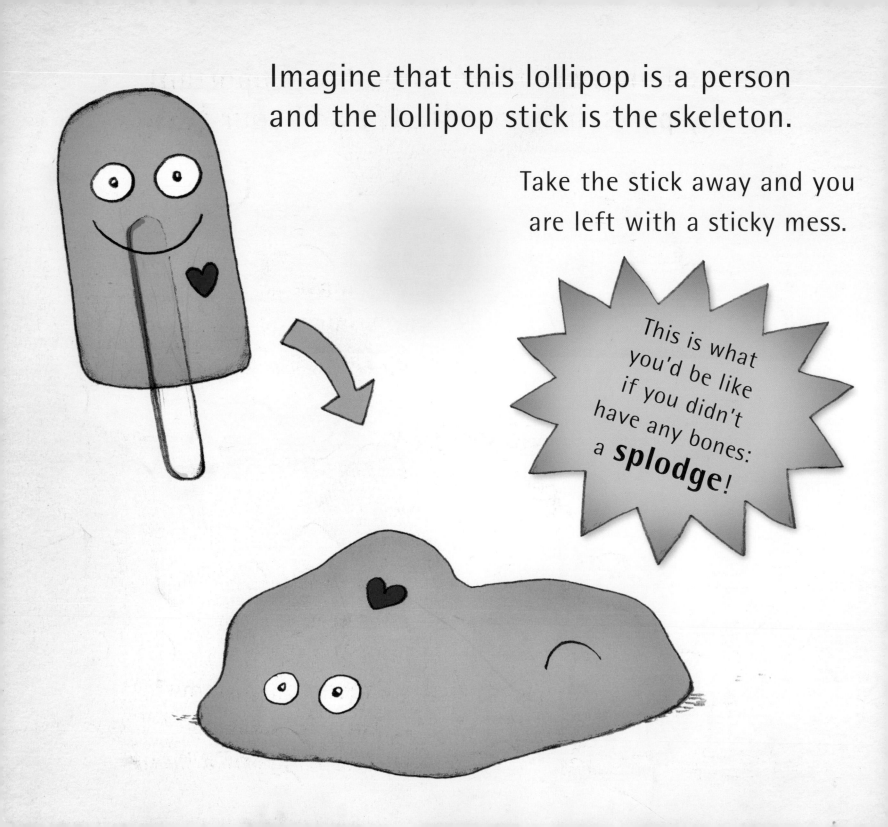

Imagine that this lollipop is a person and the lollipop stick is the skeleton.

Take the stick away and you are left with a sticky mess.

This is what you'd be like if you didn't have any bones: a **splodge**!

Some bones are there to protect important squashy parts, like your **heart** and your **lungs**.

Your ribs make a strong, bony cage to keep them **safe**.

ribs

Can you find your ribs at your sides, above your tummy? They feel like the rungs of a ladder.

The bone inside your head is called your **skull**.

skull

The skull is there to protect your brain.

Can you feel it in your head, like a helmet under the skin?

If it wasn't for your skull, your brain would slosh about inside your head, like a poached egg in a plastic bag.

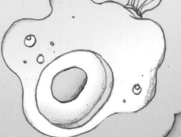

The pointy bone at your elbow is called your **funny bone**.

OUCH!

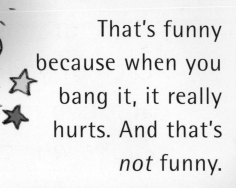

That's funny because when you bang it, it really hurts. And that's *not* funny.

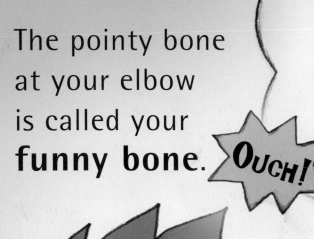

The flat bone where your leg bends is called your **kneecap**.
It feels like a little plate over your knee.

And like a plate, your knee could smash into lots of pieces if you fell on it hard. And that would really hurt!

kneecap

That's why skaters wear knee pads.

There are three bones in each of your four fingers, and two in each thumb. That's why they are so bendy.

Your smallest bone is in the **ear**.

Your longest bone is in the **thigh**.

Having lots of finger bones means that your hands can move around and do fiddly things, like:

playing the piano.

Toes don't have as many bones as fingers.
You can wiggle your toes, but you can't write with your feet – well, not without a lot of practice!

Bones are held together with special stretchy things called **ligaments**. They're like elastic bands under the skin.

The place where two bones meet is called a **joint**.

ligaments

ligaments

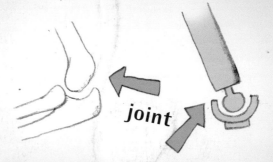

joint

Leg bones meet at the knee joint. They move backward and forward like a door.

Your legs are attached to your body at the hip joint. The joint moves around like a candy apple cupped in the palm of your hand.

KAPOW!

Sometimes joints can get worn out. This old lady had her hip replaced. Now she can do a karate kick!

Let's have a closer look at a bone:

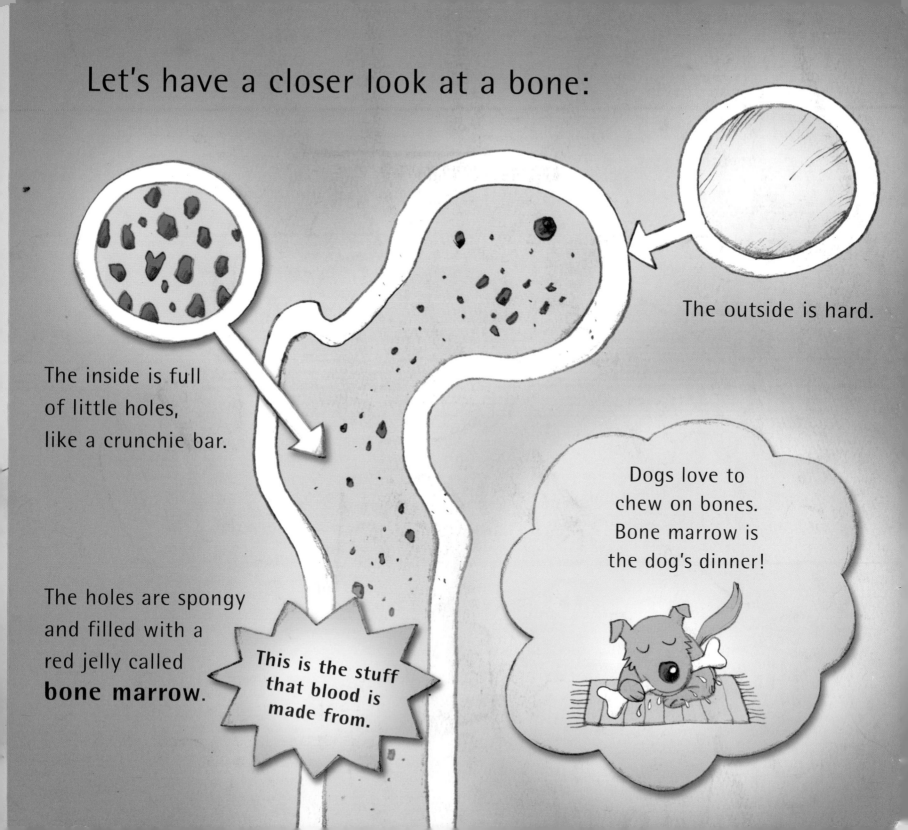

The outside is hard.

The inside is full of little holes, like a crunchie bar.

The holes are spongy and filled with a red jelly called **bone marrow**.

This is the stuff that blood is made from.

Dogs love to chew on bones. Bone marrow is the dog's dinner!

Some creatures don't have any bones at all, like:

Sharks
Their skeletons are made out of gristle, like the stuff you can feel when you press the end of your nose.

Jellyfish
They flubber about by opening and closing like an umbrella.

Slugs and worms
These creatures wriggle and slither along on muscle power.

THeY're aLL SPINELESS!

Some creatures, like insects and spiders, wear their bodies inside out!

Crabs and snails have exoskeletons, called shells, for extra protection.

If this lobster got into a fight his bones would stop him from getting too badly hurt, like a knight wearing a suit of armor.

EeeeeeeK!

Exoskeletons are waterproof, like a raincoat. That's how this spider can keep popping back up the drain.

It is possible to look at your bones without taking them out of your skin.

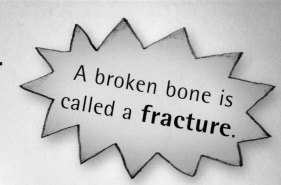

A broken bone is called a **fracture**.

A big machine can take a picture called an **X-ray**. A doctor may do this if he thinks that a bone is broken.

A small break is called a **hairline fracture**, meaning as thin as a strand of hair.

A **big** break means that the bone has snapped like a pencil!

If a bone is broken, it can mend itself.

It's wrapped in a special bandage called a **cast**. This will stop the bone from moving about so it can grow back together again.

Cast

It's a great surface for your friends to write their autographs on!

If a broken bone isn't wrapped in a cast, it might grow back in a funny position, like this!

Bones like food that contains calcium because it makes them strong.

yogurt

rice

juice

cheese

milk

broccoli

exercise

fish

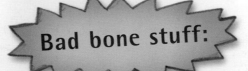
Bad bone stuff:

not wearing helmets

no exercise

sitting still for too long

lifting heavy things

slouching

jumping without bending your knees